THE STRESSED-OUT WRITER'S GUIDE TO RECORDING YOUR OWN AUDIOBOOK

BOOKS BY KIRK HANLEY

The Chandler Shott Mysteries
Shott in the Dark

The Stressed-Out Writer's Guides
The Stressed-Out Writer's Guide to Recording Your Own Audiobook

To find out more about Kirk and sign-up for his free email updates, please go to www.kirkhanley.com.

THE STRESSED-OUT WRITER'S GUIDE TO RECORDING YOUR OWN AUDIOBOOK

Kirk Hanley

Copyright © 2015 by Kirk Hanley

All rights reserved. No part of this publication may be reproduced, distributed or transmitted in any form or by any means, including photocopying, recording, or other electronic or mechanical methods, without the prior written permission of the publisher, except in the case of brief quotations embodied in critical reviews and certain other noncommercial uses permitted by copyright law. For permission requests, write to the publisher, addressed "Attention: Permissions Coordinator," at the address below.

Kirk Hanley
P.O. Box 150641
Alexandria, Virginia 22315
www.kirkhanley.com

Book Layout ©2013 BookDesignTemplates.com

The Stressed-Out Writer's Guide to Recording Your Own Audiobook / Kirk Hanley. -- 1st ed.
ISBN 978-1507665589

Table of Contents

Welcome, Stressed-Out Writer	1
So Why Listen to Me?	5
What is an Audiobook?	9
Advantages of Offering an Audiobook	15
Where Can You Distribute Your Audiobook?	19
Why Should You Narrate Your Own Book?	25
Do You Have What It Takes to Narrate a Book?	31
What Equipment Do You Need?	35
How to Set Up Audacity	45
Recording Your Audiobook	51
The First Edit – Quality Control	59
The Second Edit – Mastering	65
Putting Your Audiobook Together	75
How to Read Like a Pro	79
So Long, Stressed-Out Writer	89
Resources	91
Glossary	97
About the Author	103

Welcome, Stressed-Out Writer

There's a lot of information out there for writers today. First there are books. And thanks to the ease of self-publishing, more eBooks and print books appear on Amazon every day. Then there are blogs. And YouTube videos. And podcasts. And articles. Not to mention Facebook, Twitter, Google+, Pinterest, and on and on. It's enough to stress you out!

You know that stressed-out feeling. You want to accomplish a task but don't know which way to turn. So you do a Google search for information and find 1,345,287 results. You read a blog written by an expert, but it's so filled with jargon you have no idea what they're talking about. You buy another so-called expert's eBook and find that you know more about the topic (and basic grammar) than they do. You peruse an authority's site that seems to have the info you want, but you can only access it after you pay for their $499 eCourse. Turning away from the Internet, you go to a brick-and-mortar bookstore and find a guide that might do the trick. But it's the size of a cinder block and will take you eight hours to read...when you have eight hours of free time – which you never do – so it gathers dust on a shelf. It's enough to stress you out!

That's why I wanted to create a series of books for you, the stressed-out writer. You have a limited amount of time and a busy life outside of writing. You want to find the answers to your questions quickly and then get on with the writing life – and life itself. You don't want or need a user manual that shows the ins and outs of every last aspect of the topic with an index the size of the New York phone book. (Remember phone books?) You just want the shortest possible route from A to B, without side trips to J, Q, or W.

The Stressed-Out Writer's Guide Series is that resource. Each book is a quick read for a reasonable price. I promise to give you all the information you need to accomplish your task, without any padding intended to fill it out to some artificial length.

So before I wear out my welcome and violate my own rules on padding, one last thing: This book contains what I know on this topic to date, and gives you the information you need to get up and running quickly. But information changes. And I certainly don't know it all. That's why I intend to revise this book and create a new edition in the future. So if you want to drop me a line to ask me a question about something I didn't cover here, to let me know that a fact or procedure is out of date, or to tell me about a great new resource, I'd be eternally grateful. And if I make changes based on your input, I'll be sure to credit you in the next edition.

In any case, I sincerely hope you'll sign up for my updates here: www.kirkhanley.com. And since I hate spammers as much as you do, (maybe more so – I'm sure you're a very nice person) I will never, ever share your email with anyone else.

Enough with the yakety yak and clackety clack. On with the book...

So Why Listen to Me?

So who am I and why should you listen to me? Let me briefly introduce myself.

My name is Kirk Hanley. For over 30 years, I've been a writer, performer, and improviser. I've worked with some folks you might have heard of. As a writer, I've created headlines for The Onion News Network, co-written a spoof of office manuals for CareerBuilder, and ghostwritten articles for major magazines. For over 15 years, I worked for the renowned comedy theatre, The Second City, first in my hometown of Detroit and later in their hometown of Chicago. At Second City I produced, directed, performed, improvised, wrote, and conducted workshops. For about five years, I was head writer of Second City Communications, the business arm of Second City, where I wrote over a thousand sketches, videos, podcasts, web content, and more for organizations ranging from Fortune 500 companies to charitable foundations to mom-and-pop shops, finding the funny in everything from retreaded tires to pharmaceutical sales.

In early 2013, I started recording audiobooks through ACX, an Amazon platform that allows rightsholders to connect with narrators to produce their audiobooks. I had done voiceover work in the past, but most of what I'd done was about 30 seconds long – commercials, taglines for videos, that sort of thing. Producing audiobooks was a whole different kettle of fish (or ball of wax, for you vegans). Recording hours of audio requires a lot of stamina – and more than a little bit of planning – to ensure consistency over the course of the audiobook.

But performing wasn't what intimidated me. What really intimidated me were the ACX technical requirements. Reading a phrase like "Each uploaded file must have a noise floor no higher than –60dB RMS" is enough to make you break out in a cold sweat. (And that can short out your electronics.) So I dug in and visited forums, Googled technical terms, listened to podcasts, and learned everything I could about audio. Over time, I came up with a method for producing an audiobook that I thought would work.

I spent hours recording that first audiobook, and was a nervous wreck when I finally submitted it to ACX. I waited for three weeks to hear back, wondering if it would be approved or if ACX would send it back to me with a note saying, "Sorry, you need to record this all over again from the beginning. P.S. Please transfer the files you submitted to a CD and then break that CD in half." But they didn't. They approved it. I was overjoyed. Until I listened to the sample on the sales page, that is.

The sample had a low-level hiss running through the background. And it sounded a little echoey. Oh sure, it was listenable. But it didn't sound like the samples from the big-time publishers and voiceover superstars that buyers would be comparing me to. So I went back to the drawing board. I discovered noise cancellation. And I improved the quality of my recording space by using a sophisticated sound deadening device (a $3 bath towel). With every recording I made, I got more skilled as a narrator and each audiobook I produced sounded a little better. Today, I'd put my products up against anything the big publishers produce.

I tell you all this to alleviate the intimidation factor. I learned how to do this, and I think you can, too. I want you to benefit from my missteps. I'll lay out the method I've developed for producing an audiobook that will pass ACX's standards, but more importantly, will meet your personal standards of producing a high-quality audio version of your book.

Are there those who will criticize my methodology? You bet. Outside of political forums, there is no more opinionated group on the Internet than those in the audio world. Some will say you can use a $100 microphone and others say to do things right you need a $1000 microphone. There are those who say *always* normalize your recording and those who say you must *never* normalize. Those who say you should always apply noise cancellation versus those who wonder why you want to ruin your recording. Those who say only a real hack would a) remove breaths or b) leave breaths in. It is literally impossible to follow all the conflicting advice out there.

So in this guide, I'll share with you the method I use to efficiently create a great sounding recording, with a solid performance, using reasonably priced equipment. That means you'll produce an audiobook you can take pride in – without getting stressed-out.

What is an Audiobook?

Seems like a lot of authors I've encountered on ACX have never listened to an audiobook in their lives. I can tell, because they put all sorts of requirements on the project page they create for auditions. They want a different narrator for male and female characters. Or they want an entire cast of people. Music is required, of course. I saw one that said they wanted the narrator to deliver a read that was "angry throughout the whole book." (No, you really don't.)

Besides being control freaks (perhaps an occupational hazard for self-published authors), I think some authors often have audiobooks confused with audio dramas or old radio shows. Don't get me wrong – these are great. But they're not audiobooks. To oversimplify, audio dramas are to audiobooks as screenplays are to novels. An audio drama is written as such. It is more or less an audio version of a stage play, without the benefit of visuals. That's why some of the more hackneyed old radio plays used to have dialogue like: "Look. In front of us. It's a door. I'm going to reach out and turn the knob. I'm pushing it open. Oh look, it's another room." (I'm exaggerating for comic effect – but just barely.)

An audiobook, on the other hand, is a print book brought to life by a narrator, with all the description, exposition, dialogue, and even dialogue attributions included. Every word in the original book is read aloud. People who haven't listened to an entire audiobook ask, "How does that work?" and "Isn't that boring?" (The answers are "Very well" and "No, not if it's done right.") Of course, in nonfiction it's mostly information, often without dialogue, but it works just as well.

Ideally, when you listen to an audiobook, the narrator sort of falls away from your consciousness and the experience becomes the same as if you were reading the print book yourself. A good narrator makes subtle changes to his tone, inflection, pace, and pitch to differentiate between characters, mimicking the inner voice of a reader. It can sometimes take a few minutes to enter this "waking dream," but when you do, you are fully immersed in the story and it unfolds before you, making for an experience every bit as enjoyable as – and sometimes even more so than – the actual experience of reading a book yourself. If you listen to an audiobook on a long car trip, you'll understand what I mean. The miles literally fly by.

A skilled narrator is important, but not always essential. One of the most memorable audiobooks I ever listened to was by Dave Thomas, founder of Wendy's, reading his autobiography, *Dave's Way*. When it comes to dramatically interpreting the written word...let's just say Dave makes a great hamburger. But his life story was so engrossing that his rather clunky presentation didn't detract from it at all, but was actually quite charming. Later on, I'll give you some tips that the pros use to help you with your delivery. But know that your readers will cut you some slack if you're not a pro, and will appreciate hearing the words read in the voice of the author as a way to connect with you.

I would suggest that before you record your first audiobook – or even hire someone else to narrate your audiobook – that you listen to a few samples. If you're old school, you can head down to your local library and pick up some books on CD (or even books on tape if you're *old*, old school.) Or you can download an mp3 from Amazon or Audible. Audible even has a deal where you can get your first audiobook for free.

Almost any audiobook put out by one of the major publishing houses is going to be high quality and read by an experienced narrator, so go ahead and pick up one of those books you've been meaning to read and instead, listen to it on your commute, while walking the dog, or when working out at the gym. But try to choose a book narrated by someone you've never heard of. If you choose one narrated by a movie star or television actor it will no doubt be good, but knowing too much about their personal life or other roles they've played will tend to take you out of the story. Not to mention, the folks who aren't household names make their living narrating audiobooks and have dozens, sometimes hundreds, of titles under their belts. They are hired time and time again not because their star quality will boost sales, but because they're great at what they do.

To get an idea what different narrators sound like, you can listen to samples online. Samples are usually less than five minutes in length, but you'll often find yourself drawn in despite the brevity, and be disappointed when the sample ends, wanting to hear more. It's almost like they want you to buy the rest of the book. (Hey, wait a minute...)

To find free samples online, simply go to the Amazon or Audible website and search for titles within your favorite genre. Chances are there will be an audio version of any book that is a bestseller. Click on the sample button and it will play automatically in your browser. Another great source of samples, along with an overview of what's going on in the audiobook market, is the digital version of AudioFile magazine, which you can find at:

digital.audiofilemagazine.com

Here you can listen to samples of audiobooks, read up on who's who and what's what in the audiobook industry, and listen to a whole slew of different narrators, all in one convenient place.

Advantages of Offering an Audiobook

Recording and producing an audiobook can be quite a labor- and time-intensive process. So why bother?

The truth is you don't have to. Many authors live out successful careers without ever recording their own audiobooks or having someone else do it for them. But there are still a number of advantages to consider.

First, it is an additional revenue stream. Authors, especially self-published authors, need to look at every possible way to exploit their rights and make their works work for them. The list that every author should consider includes eBooks, paperbacks, foreign sales, translations, apps, and audiobooks. Every item on this list may not be appropriate for you and your individual situation, but each should be examined in terms of creating a new income stream from an existing work.

And audiobooks, once recorded, are a largely passive income source. In other words, you produce the product once, and it continues to create income for you for years, with little to no additional effort on your part. Even though you should consider some marketing, a lot of it is done for you, since customers viewing your book on Amazon will see your audiobook listed with the other versions. And those who like listening to audiobooks frequent Audible and iTunes looking for the next great author.

Audiobooks are one of the fastest growing segments of the book market. And with people beginning to listen to audiobooks on their smartphones, computers, and other electronic devices, there's no end in sight. Conversely, audiobooks are a far less competitive market for self-published authors, since only a fraction of books become audiobooks. For example, ACX says that in 2009 there were 100,000 books published, but only 5000 were turned into audiobooks. Less competition translates into better discoverability, meaning your audiobook has a chance to break out.

Finally, having an audiobook puts you in a different class of author. You've probably perused the listings on Amazon and seen a book that was only available in a Kindle edition. I don't know about you but, fairly or unfairly, the fact that there is not a print edition always makes me question if it's a "real book." Does that mean it's not a good book, or not a worthwhile read? Of course not. But having your book in print, eBook, and audio definitely puts you in a different class of author and makes you look like a professional who takes your business seriously.

Not to mention, there will be hardcore fans who want to buy every version of your work. And why deprive them of the ability to give their money to you?

Where Can You Distribute Your Audiobook?

When it comes to distribution, it's helpful to think about the audio version of a book the same way you think about the book itself. A book consists of words. If you want folks to read your words, there are a number of ways to deliver those words to them. You can create an eBook and publish it through an online bookstore such as Amazon, Barnes and Noble, iTunes, etc. You can make it into an app and put it up on GooglePlay or iTunes. Or you can make a print book and publish it through CreateSpace, Lulu, or any print on demand service. You can make a pdf and sell it directly on your website. You could even do it the way we did it back in the day by going down to your local print shop and having them copy it and put a spiral binding on it. Each of these methods has its pluses and minuses, but whichever way you choose to distribute your words, the content remains the same.

An audiobook is simply the recorded audio version of your words. You could put out an mp3 of the recording and sell it directly on your website. You could burn the files onto a CD and sell it through the mail or at conferences, or stick it into the paperback version of your physical book. You could put the book up as a podcast on iTunes or SoundCloud. Or you could submit your mp3 files through ACX and have the service distribute your audiobook and put it up for sale on Amazon, Audible, and iTunes.

Again, each of these methods have their advantages and disadvantages. But if you want to reach the largest number of listeners with the least work on your part, I would suggest you handle your distribution through ACX.

What is ACX?

ACX is short for the Audiobook Creation Exchange. It is an Amazon platform that allows rightsholders in the US and UK to connect with producers who can narrate and create their audiobook. (If you are a traditionally published author, you'll need to check with your publisher to see who has the audio rights. Chances are, it's not you.) It is a sort of eBay for audiobooks where "buyers" (authors of books) can put up samples of their work for audition from "sellers" (audiobook producers). The marketplace is free to all involved. ACX handles file storage, conversion, and customer fulfillment. They put the audiobook up for sale on Amazon, Audible, and iTunes and create the sales pages. A team of experts check all files submitted for quality and sound levels. In addition to distributing audiobooks, they host a blog where they share information about voiceover, being an author, and being a narrator. They also offer free tutorials on the website to help you learn the ins and outs of audio production. And they have a very helpful support staff that can assist when you have problems.

Let's talk about that term "producer." When major publishers hire folks to narrate their audiobooks, that's all they hire: a narrator. Voiceover performers show up at a recording studio where an audio engineer and a producer work. The studio supplies all the audio equipment. The voiceover performer enters a little padded booth (that's right, they're sent to a padded room), puts on headphones, and stands in front of a microphone. There's a little window where the performer can see the engineer and producer, who sit in the main room of the studio. The engineer works at a computer monitor and adjusts the microphone, sound levels, equalizers, and other equipment in order to produce audio files with the best possible sound. The producer is there to listen to the words, act as an independent ear, and give notes on character, watch for mistakes, and in general, make sure the interpretation is the best representation of the author's intent. Usually, the recording process doesn't involve the author at all.

When ACX came along, they required actors to become narrator, engineer, and producer all rolled into one, under the title "producer." Suddenly, performers like me, who were used to just showing up and reading, had to learn about audio recording software, dB levels, clip rates, and the like.

When authors put their works up for audition on ACX, they decide whether they want to pay the producer once, outright, or do a royalty split. If they decide to pay directly, they set a rate per finished hour, which is just what it sounds like. If an author agrees to pay $100 per finished hour and the final audio book is 6.5 hours, they would pay the producer $650. The author is then free to distribute the audiobook exclusively through ACX, or to take a smaller royalty and distribute it through ACX and elsewhere.

If the author decides to do a royalty split, then he or she owes the narrator no money up front. Instead the author and narrator split a royalty (currently 40%) based on the sales price and agree to distribute the audiobook exclusively through ACX. So if the audiobook sells for $10, the author and producer split $4 between them. In other words, they receive $2 each. (It isn't really quite this simple, since some royalties are based on a price calculated by Audible using a membership model, but let's not get bogged down at this point.) ACX determines the sales price, taking into account the length, and the author and producer have no say in the matter. In addition, ACX offers a bounty of $50, split evenly between the author and producer, each time your audiobook is the first purchase of a new Audible member. This money is paid in addition to the royalty, and there is no limit to how many bounties can be earned.

If an author so desires, they can act as their own producer and keep the entire 40% royalty and $50 bounties for themselves. Of course, that means being author, narrator, engineer, and producer. (As if you didn't have enough jobs as a self-publisher already!) We'll discuss why you might want to act as your own narrator and producer in the next chapter.

To sign up for ACX, go to www.acx.com and click on "How It Works." You'll find a step-by-step process for creating an account, claiming the audio rights for your book, and then exercising those rights to create a new audiobook project.

Why Should You Narrate Your Own Book?

Hopefully by this time you see the value in having an audiobook version of your work. But since you can go through ACX and find an experienced producer to do the narration and technical mastery of your book through a royalty deal, with no up-front expense on your part, why not just do that and be done? You won't get an argument from me. After all, I make a big part of my living doing just that, and far be it from me to look a gift horse in the mouth, bite the hand that feeds me, or any other cliché you'd like to throw at it.

But if you're an author working in your lonely garret (Do you have a garret? If so, send me a picture for my upcoming blog, "A Garret of My Own.") it may freak you out a bit, this idea of collaborating with a producer. Working with others can bring you new ideas, new opportunities, and new contacts. But the downside is that you have to depend on someone else to meet deadlines, you may choose someone whose sensibilities or work habits are completely different than your own, and you have to share the credit (and the cash). Plus, recording your own book has its advantages. Let's take a look.

If you have loyal readers, they want to find ways to connect with you. That's why we're all on social media these days – to connect with readers. Hearing the sound of your voice and your interpretation of the text will really appeal to a lot of your hardcore fans. And to your non-hardcore fans, it signals that you care a great deal about your work, that you didn't just write a book and throw it up online to see what would happen. Plus not everyone is familiar with the audiobook market – frankly, hearing the book read by the author is what many people expect.

The truth is, no one knows your own book better than you. You may have a certain actor or archetype in mind for one of your characters. If you hand off your book to an actor, even a great actor, he may take an entirely different approach or interpretation. If in your mind the hero of your epic novel is Matthew McConaughey, but the narrator reads him like he's Pee-wee Herman, you are going to be sorely disappointed. For 200 pages.

Another reason to read your own audiobook is one that might not be apparent to you at first glance. Reading your own work will make you a better writer. Between editing, quality control, and mastering (don't panic – we'll cover these in depth later on) you can end up reading and/or listening to the same passages three or four times. And after a while, you can begin to hate them a little bit. Think you're critical of your writing now? Wait until you read it aloud. You will learn some positive things about your writing: What your strengths are, who your characters are, where the pace of your work increases and decreases. You'll also learn some not-so-positive things: Where you've used run-on sentences, awkward sentence construction, repetitive phrases, and so forth. Every mistake and cliché that your eye glided smoothly over when writing, will be like nails on a chalkboard to your ear (to use another cliché). And if it's been a while since you committed the words to paper (or electrons) you'll sometimes come across a sentence that really trips you up, one that you have no idea how to say aloud. And you wrote it! Humbling. Of course, some sentences that are grammatically correct and make sense on paper just do not read well, such as when ordinary words combine to create tongue twisters. But sometimes, let's face it, it's just bad writing.

So if you get nothing else out of this book, please take this away: Even if you decide recording your own audiobook and sending it out into the world is not for you, reading your own work aloud in the quiet of your room should always be the final step in the proofreading process. Reading aloud, you'll find typos that your eye skips over. You'll discover awkward sentence construction, repetitive words, dialogue mis-attributed to characters, and unnecessary words. The truth is, a lot of readers really do read the book aloud in their own head or by silently moving their lips. And those readers will get tripped up by the same things that trip you up when reading aloud. The last thing you want is for readers to have to reread passages just to have them make sense. Every time a reader has to stop or go back, it breaks the spell and pulls them out of the story. No one wants that.

If you record your book and find the process enjoyable, you may even be able to add another source of income to your portfolio by becoming a narrator for other people's books. Authors trust other authors to treat their work with care and respect. And maybe you're just the person to do it. With the audiobook market expanding at a faster rate than the publishing industry as a whole, being a narrator is a skill that is sure to be in demand for years to come and can help you make some income when sales of your own books are slow. If nothing else, you'll have the equipment and expertise to record not only audiobooks, but also podcasts, YouTube video presentations, audio for eCourses, and much more.

Of course, this means you will also have to learn the technical side of things. And I won't sugarcoat it – there is a learning curve. But I'll lead you through the production process I use step-by-step, so you don't have to go through the trial and error I did. Before you know it, you'll have your first audiobook out and on sale where your friends, family, and even (hopefully) total strangers can buy it. So then when people give you that old tired excuse that they don't have time to sit down and read your book, you can tell them: "No problem, you can listen to it anytime you want. I'll even read it to you."

Do You Have What It Takes to Narrate a Book?

So, perhaps I've whetted your appetite to record your own book. But do you have what it takes to be an audiobook narrator? The truth is, you never know until you try. Fortunately doing a scratch recording is easy, free, and relatively painless. And it's a good idea to try this before investing in equipment or signing up with ACX.

Grab any cheap digital recorder. You can probably find a digital recording app already installed on your cell phone or just search iTunes or the Google Play store for one – the simpler to use the better. Next take a copy of your book – or any favorite book – and read it aloud into your recording device. Imagine you're at a staged reading at a bookstore, or you're reading a passage to your significant other, family member, or friend. At this point, don't worry too much about characters and inflection. Just have fun with it and get used to the act of reading aloud. If you don't have young children, you may not have read aloud for years. Read for about five minutes and then take a listen.

You will probably hate the sound of your own voice. Almost everyone does the first time they hear it. There is a physiological explanation for this phenomenon. Normally when we speak, we don't hear our voice through only our ears. Our voice also vibrates through the bones of our body and up to our ears from the inside, pumping up the bass and making it sound richer. The first time we hear our voice the way others do, it's a bit disconcerting. It's our voice, but it's not "us."

There's a psychological aspect at play here as well. We are always more suave and debonair in our minds than we are in actuality. When we hear that nasally miscreant speaking, we are horrified. But don't worry. Everyone feels this way. With time and experience, you'll eventually make peace with the sound of your recorded voice and be able to divorce yourself (slightly) from the self-judgment. You'll listen to your voice more objectively, as you would the sound of someone else's voice.

Next we should talk endurance. Roughly 10,000 words of text translates into one finished hour of audio. So do a word count on your book and divide by 10,000 to get an approximate finished time for your audiobook in hours. But realize that one finished hour will actually take you between 90 minutes and two hours to record. Why? You'll make mistakes and have to rerecord. You'll trip over your own tongue. You'll record a line and not like your cadence or intonation or interpretation, and take a second pass at it. All of which adds to your recording time. You'll get better over time, but there will never be a one-to-one correspondence between recorded hours and finished hours. No one is that good – we're all human.

Unless you write very short books, you will find recording your book to be a marathon. So your next assignment is to try and read an entire book aloud. Start with a shorter one, say less than 200 pages. Lock the door to your office or sit in your car and read aloud. No fair cheating by just moving your lips or whispering. You want to use the same muscles you would use when recording – muscles in your face and jaw, your diaphragm, your tongue, your vocal cords. You want to see if you're able to maintain your breath when reading long sentences. You want to see how your vocal cords stand up to constant use.

You don't have to read the whole book in one sitting. You won't have to do that when actually recording. But try to read for at least an hour at a time, uninterrupted. With practice, you will get better and build endurance. But if you have physical limitations that prevent you from recording a book-length manuscript, it's better to find that out sooner rather than later. There may be things you can do to improve your vocal endurance. You can take voice lessons, or practice deep breathing. I used to almost lose my voice after a relatively short period of recording. It would get very thin and weak. Turns out it was allergies. My doctor recommended an over-the-counter allergy medication, and now I'm able to read for quite some time without any degradation in my voice.

If you've gotten this far, let's go back to the recorder and work on technique. Practice reading a short passage once again. Try different interpretations – don't worry if they don't make sense. Read with different emotions – anger, sadness, longing. Try speaking as if you're addressing a crowd and then try it as if you're speaking to a close friend. Try reading very fast, as fast as you can, followed by reading as slowly as you can stand. Try reading as different characters – a cowboy, a socialite, a bratty kid – whatever you interpret each of these characters to be. Try reading as you imagine different family members, friends, and coworkers might sound, or do your best impression of a celebrity. The point of this exercise is this: These are the skills you must use to keep an audiobook interesting for both you and the listener. You need to vary your pace. You need to create characters. You need to make your reading as intimate as you can. They're skills you can work on, but if all this is falling on deaf ears or just seems stupid, then your performance may not be as effective as it could be.

If you've gotten this far, congratulations! If this seems like fun, then you're a good candidate for reading your own book. If it wasn't exactly fun, but didn't make you want to quit...well, we can work with that too.

What Equipment Do You Need?

In this chapter I'll tell you what equipment I use to record. My entire setup cost me less than $100. Prices go up and down, but I imagine you'll still be able to do it for around that same figure. Can you spend more and get better equipment? Certainly. And if you spend any time reading audio forums or researching recommendations on ACX, you'll find folks recommending setups ranging into the hundreds – and even thousands – of dollars. You see, for the audio geeks out there, no matter how much you spend on microphones and how much sound deadening foam you surround yourself with, you will never quite reach the pinnacle of noise-reducing, bass-optimized, dB-equalized perfection. To tell you the truth, I can't make heads or tails of most of it – and I have an engineering degree! So take my advice: Do your due diligence, learn the basics, and always be thinking of ways to upgrade your setup, aiming toward improvement. But don't make yourself crazy.

Let's be realistic – we're talking about audiobooks here, not recording the next hot R&B single on the top 100s chart. Most people listen to their audiobooks through tiny ear buds while riding the subway, or through the speaker on their phone while walking the crowded streets of the city, or through their car speakers while driving in rush hour traffic. Does that mean you shouldn't try to make a quality sound recording, free from background noise? Of course not, but it isn't rocket science. Far more important is the quality of your performance, something we'll address later.

The Microphone

There are two broad categories of microphone: Condenser and dynamic. A condenser microphone requires an external power source. For a home studio, this means you have to run a cable from your microphone to a piece of equipment called an audio interface and then run another cable from your audio interface to your computer. If you're trying to combine two or three microphones into one recording – such as when you're doing an interview or panel discussion – then an audio interface is a great piece of equipment to have. But for our purposes, it unnecessarily complicates things when there are high-quality dynamic microphones that you can connect directly to your computer using a USB plug. Some audiophiles claim that a condenser microphone gives you better sound and dynamic range, but I've never been able to hear it. That doesn't mean it isn't true, just that to the casual listener, it really doesn't make a huge difference. Each and every microphone, regardless of category and type, will have different audio characteristics, so you may want to experiment with a few and see which one works best with your voice. But if you want to get up and running quickly with a quality microphone for a reasonable price, I'll give you my recommendation.

The microphone I use is the Audio-Technica ATR2100-USB Cardioid Dynamic USB/XLR Microphone. I did a fair amount of research before purchasing a mic and most every review, even by experienced podcasters and techie types, agreed that the ATR2100 was every bit as good as microphones costing $200 or more. When I purchased my ATR2100 through Amazon, it cost $37. At the time of this writing, it's selling for a bit more – on Amazon it's around $60. (Check around the web and you may be able to get an even better price.) But even at that price it's still a huge bargain compared to microphones of similar quality. It even comes with a little tripod stand, which, while not the most robust one I've ever seen, will work nicely for a desktop setup.

In addition to the microphone, you'll want to get some sort of windscreen or pop filter. Strictly speaking, these aren't necessary, but they can make a difference if you have a tendency to pop your plosives (letters such as p or t). There is a freestanding pop filter, which is a piece of thin mesh material stretched inside a small metal ring, attached to an adjustable arm with a screw-in mounting bracket. In my experience, this type of pop filter can be a bit cumbersome, and occasionally your hand may hit the arm, ruining a take. Cheaper and simpler is a windscreen, which is a small foam sleeve that fits directly over the microphone head. This typically costs just a few dollars and will do the trick nicely.

Mini Sound Booth

One of the biggest obstacles to a good performance is ambient room noise. In a professional voiceover recording studio, you enter a small room lined with foam panels to stop sound from bouncing around, creating what is known as a "dead room." If you've ever entered a small walk-in closet packed with clothes, you've experienced this same effect. (Incidentally, if you can locate your voiceover studio in a small walk-in closet packed with clothes, that can be an ideal set-up.) If not, let's take a look at how we can recreate that same effect in a normal room. Of course, the smaller the room and the fewer hard surfaces, the better. Basically, you want to avoid that big, echoey, empty room sound. And you'll want to stay away from rooms with windows overlooking busy streets, construction sites, marching band practice fields, etc.

But even if you don't have an ideal room and if space in your crowded life is at a premium, there's a lot we can do to recreate the audio characteristics of that professional voiceover booth on a budget. I credit this idea to voiceover guru Harlan Hogan, but was able to execute it on the cheap. The idea is recreate the characteristics of that dead room, by deadening the space surrounding your microphone.

To do that, we'll create a mini sound booth by placing the microphone inside a foam-lined box. The type of box doesn't matter much, but one about 1 foot by 1 foot by 1 foot will do the job nicely and take up little more space on your desktop than your microphone does on its own. The box I bought at Target is a black plastic storage cube and cost me about $14. There are also soft-sided storage cubes and some that collapse, but unless you intend to take your setup on trips, I think you'll prefer something solid you can set your script on when you work.

Next you'll want to line the five inner sides of the box with pyramid acoustic foam, which is exactly what it sounds like: foam with raised pyramids on one side. There are a few different varieties, but don't get too hung up here. As long as it's called pyramid acoustic foam you should be good. The pyramids come in 1 inch, 2 inch and 3 inch heights. Choose the 2 inch foam as a nice compromise between performance and space considerations. Type the search term "pyramid acoustic foam" into Google and shop around to get the best price. I bought all the foam I needed from a seller on eBay for a total of about $20. Sometimes people sell small panels and other times supply large sheets which you can cut up yourself with scissors. You want enough foam to make five panels about 1 foot by 1 foot each.

To assemble your mini sound booth, place the cube on its side with the opening facing you. Place one foam panel at the back of your cube and line the four sides of the cube with the other foam panels, trimming as needed. In my setup, the foam panels jammed in there nicely and hold themselves in place, but you could secure them to the cube with double-sided tape if you like. Place your microphone on its stand inside the cube facing out through the opening.

RECORDING YOUR OWN AUDIOBOOK | 41

Now that we've treated the space behind, above, below, and to the left and right of the microphone, we just have to deaden the space that the microphone faces. I do this with a very sophisticated piece of equipment which I just happened to have already lying around: a thick bath towel. When I record, I have my foam box on my desk, and I clip my towel to a shelf above me and drape it over my head and shoulders, creating a snug little cocoon of acoustically deadened space.

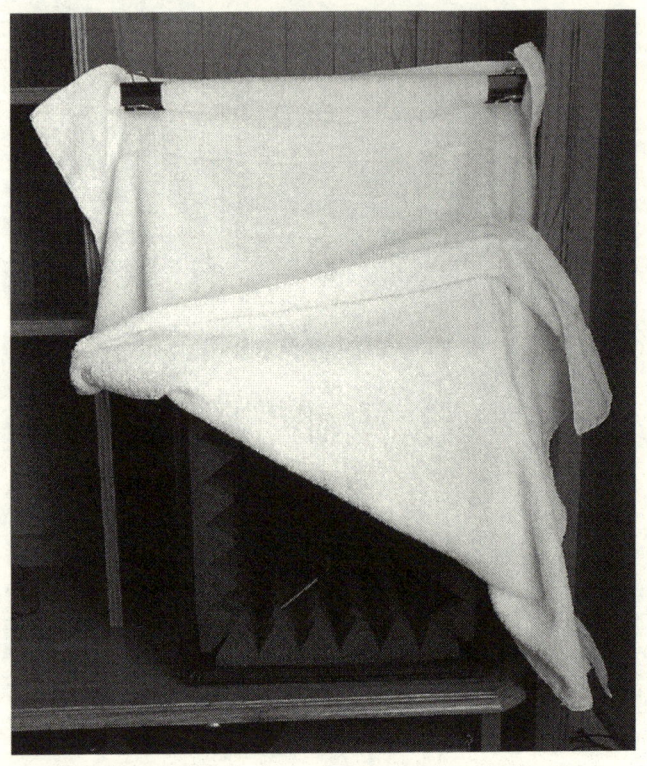

Recording and Editing Software

There are a variety of software packages out there that can help you record and edit your audiobook. Some of them cost hundreds of dollars and are designed to be used by audio engineers to record multi-track music. This is like buying a Sherman tank to take trips to the grocery store. Sure it would work, but it's overkill.

Fortunately there is a solution and best of all, it's free. Audacity is powerful audio recording and editing software that will do everything you need to produce a high-quality, great sounding, professionally edited audiobook. And since it's time-tested, it has a vibrant, active community on the web that is there to answer your questions, provide tutorials, supply plug-ins, etc. I use Audacity on a PC, but it is also available for Mac. In the next chapter, we'll take a look at Audacity and how to set it up.

How to Set Up Audacity

Audacity is a free, open-source software program for PC and Mac OS X which lets you record and edit audio and add effects. You can download the latest version by going to:

www.audacityteam.org

Follow the download instructions for your platform.

Audacity will need a few simple tweaks before you begin using it. First you need to install the LAME encoder in order to export mp3 files using Audacity. You can download the latest version by going to:

lame.buanzo.org

Follow the instructions for your platform.

Next, you'll need two plug-ins for Audacity to make the job of editing easier. The first is a tool called Chris's Dynamic Compressor. You can find it here:

theaudacitytopodcast.com/chriss-dynamic-compressor-plugin-for-audacity

The next plug-in you'll need to install is RMS Calculate. You can find it here:

forum.audacityteam.org/viewtopic.php?f=17&t=55229#p136369

Once you've downloaded the plug-in files, installing them couldn't be easier. Simply place each plug-in folder inside the Audacity installation folder on your computer and enable it. Go to:

wiki.audacityteam.org/wiki/Download_Nyquist_Plug-ins

Follow the instructions for your platform.
Now we're ready to take a look at the program. Before you open the program for the first time, plug your microphone into an open USB port on your computer. (If you plug in your microphone after you open the program, many times it will not be available as a choice. Just one of Audacity's little quirks.)
If you've never used Audacity, the screen can be a bit overwhelming at first, but don't worry. Audacity is a powerful program with a lot of options, but you'll only be using a few of the menus and features. And like any

program, after you've used it a few times, it will become second nature.

Here is a quick look at the Project Window:

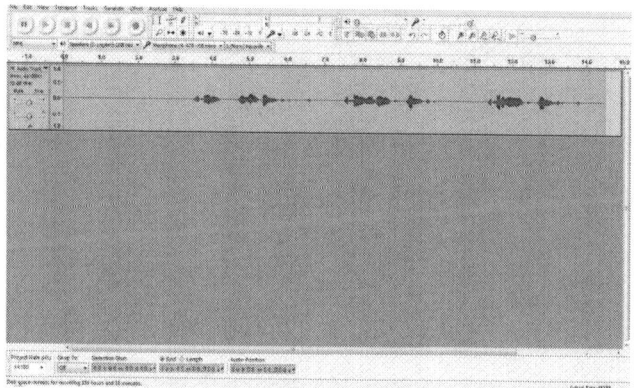

Let's handle some of the basic settings required by ACX. Once you set these you should never need to touch them again.

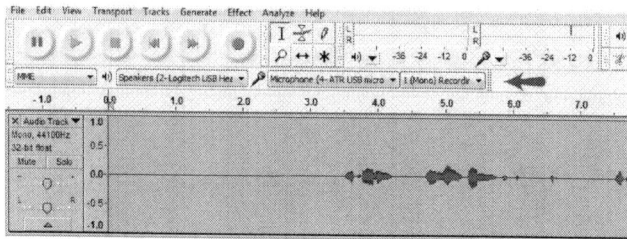

In the Device Toolbar set the first item, "Audio Host," as MME. The second item, "Playback Device," lets you choose the device you'll use to listen to your Audacity files while editing. You could listen through the speakers on your computer, but it is much better to listen to your audio files on a good pair of headphones. These don't have to be expensive, but ideally they should fit snugly on your ears to block out much of the ambient noise around you. If you have a lot of background noise in your recording, you won't notice it if you're listening in a room containing the same background noise. Good headphones will also help you to identify any minor noises such as papers turning or lip smacking so you can eliminate them and create the very best recording you can.

The third menu item lets you choose your "Recording Device" or microphone. If this is the ATR2100 I recommended earlier, this should read "4-ATR USB microphone." The final menu item allows you to choose your "Recording Channels." This should be set to "1 (Mono) Recording Channel." (Alternatively, these items can also be set under the Edit menu by choosing Preferences: Devices.)

Finally, in the Audacity Selection Toolbar, we'll set the first item, "Project Rate (Hz)," to "44100." (Alternatively, these items can also be set under the Edit menu by choosing Preferences: Quality.)

Recording Your Audiobook

Your Manuscript

You'll want to think about practicalities here. If you're using the setup I discussed earlier, you'll be sitting under a towel while you read. That means if you use a printout of your book, you'll need a source of light under there as well. But since a towel is a pretty good insulator and most light sources give off heat, pretty soon you'll find yourself sweating. Not to mention space is tight, which means turning pages will be almost impossible to do quietly, and the microphone picks up everything.

You could go without the towel. I recorded my first few books this way and they were all accepted by ACX, but the quality of the sound is just not as good. Alternatively, you could use that walk-in closet we discussed earlier or surround yourself with foam panels attached to your walls and ceiling.

But the best solution I found when using the towel was to read from my 7-inch tablet. It is lit from within, so I don't have to worry about external light sources. And I can enlarge the text as well. Plus printing out all that paper as I did in the beginning seems environmentally irresponsible (and expensive). I bought my tablet specifically for the job of recording audiobooks, but I've found so many additional uses for it that I've never regretted the purchase. You could also use your smartphone, depending on the screen size. Again, you can make the text larger within the Kindle app. But with the smaller screen size you'll find yourself turning pages more often, which can tend to throw off your rhythm.

When it's time to record, I set my tablet on top of my mini sound booth and open my document. I use Dropbox to store my manuscript files in pdf form, and open them using the Kindle app.

File Naming Conventions

When you upload your audiobook to ACX, you'll submit each chapter as a separate mp3 file, so that's also the best way to organize your Audacity projects. I name each file with the title of the book, followed by the chapter number. So for my novel, *Shott in the Dark*, the name of my first chapter's audio file would be "Shott in the Dark - Chapter 1." When I begin editing, I save a second version of the file, appending the name: "Shott in the Dark - Chapter 1 Post". The reason for creating a second file is so that in case you screw something up in editing, you'll still have the raw audio file to fall back on.

Mic Placement

When recording, you want to be as close to your microphone as you can be. A good distance is about 4 to 6 inches. An easy way to estimate this distance is to open your hand and spread your fingers out. If you put your thumb at your lips and your pinky near the front surface of the microphone, that's about right. Make sure the microphone is pointed toward your mouth along its main axis. If you find when recording that you have a challenge with plosives (letters like p or t) or breathing into your mic, it is perfectly acceptable to place your mic a bit to the side. Just be sure to angle it towards your mouth along its main axis.

Consistency is essential. You want to create a consistent configuration for where you place the mic and where you place yourself relative to the mic. Unless your book is quite short, you'll find that you need to do multiple recording sessions. The quality of your voice can vary from day to day, so you want to control what you can. Using the same configuration will help produce a more consistent sound from session to session.

Additionally, from time to time you'll need to do pickups. A pickup is the rerecording of a word or sentence because of a technical glitch, because you used the wrong word, because you put the em-PHA-sis on the wrong syl-LA-ble, or any number of other reasons. And when you have to record a pickup – as you inevitably will – you want the newly recorded audio to match the sound of what comes before and after as seamlessly as possible, so as not to pull your reader out of the story.

RECORDING YOUR OWN AUDIOBOOK | 55

Playback and Recording

In the Audacity Transport Toolbar, you'll see your playback and recording controls. Mostly you'll be working with the Record Button (the round red dot on the right), the Play Button (the green arrow second from the left), and the Stop Button (the gray square near the middle). If you prefer keyboard shortcuts, press R to record and use the spacebar to toggle between play and stop.

Recording Settings

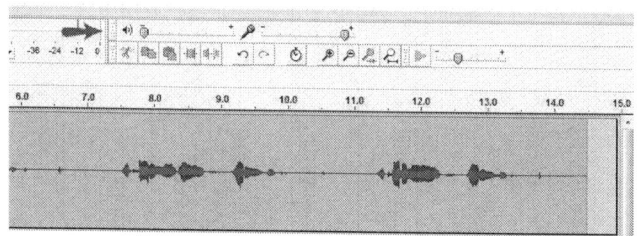

In the Audacity Mixer Toolbar, you'll see two slider controls, one for Playback Volume and one for Recording Volume. Playback Volume controls the volume of the recording when you're listening to it on your headphones or speakers. (This doesn't affect the sound levels within the recording itself.) Recording Volume controls the levels of your microphone. Slide the controller to the 0.9 position (almost all the way to the right). Then do a test recording and look at the Recording Levels in the Audacity Meter Toolbar.

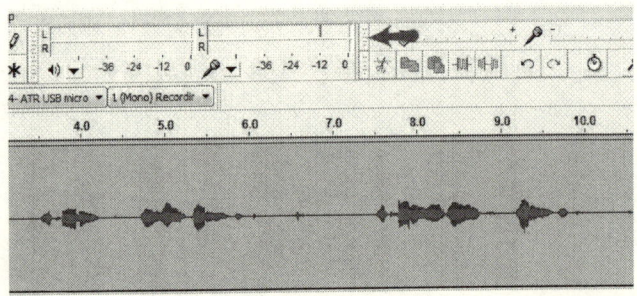

The Recording Level should be reaching almost to the top of the range, somewhere between -12dB and 0dB, when you're at your loudest. You don't want to "top out" to 0dB too much though, as this may create distortion in your recording. Adjust your Input Volume up or down, until you're consistently topping out between -12dB and 0dB. It will take a bit of experimentation, but once you get your levels set for a particular physical configuration, you will rarely need to play with them again.

Tips for Recording

I try to read an entire chapter in a single recording session, unless they are super long, say over 10,000 words. A good rule of thumb is 10,000 words will take about 90 minutes to two hours to record and will translate to roughly one hour of finished audio. This is because, as we discussed earlier, recording audio is not a completely efficient process. You'll get better, of course, but in your early sessions you'll be getting used to Audacity (and, frankly, to the whole idea of reading aloud) and that means it will take you longer to record a chapter. Be patient with yourself and you will get better – that is one guarantee I can confidently make.

Realize that the recording session is merely raw material for what will be your final audio product. And just as you would never show someone the rough draft of your manuscript, likewise, the raw audio is for you and you alone. You will be editing later – remind yourself of this often. If you stumble over a word, who cares? Just go back to the beginning of the sentence and record it again.

This can in fact be freeing. If you're not quite sure how something should be read, try it a few different ways, all in a row. For example, one of your characters is claiming ignorance by saying "I don't know." Try an innocent, honest "I don't know" followed by a defensive "I don't know!" and then a thoughtful, introspective "I don't know..." Later, when you're editing, choose the one you like best. You won't want to do this every time for every sentence, but it can be a useful technique.

The important thing is to hit the Record Button and then just keep reading. If you keep stopping the recording session and starting over, you'll never find your rhythm. Remember, it's not a live performance – you can have as many takes as you want. Relax, have fun, and it will shine through in your audiobook.

The First Edit – Quality Control

After you've recorded a chapter of your book, it's time to edit the audio file. I do two edits on the file. The first pass is strictly an edit for quality control. Did I say everything correctly? Did I stumble over anything? Were there any technical glitches that need to be fixed? Also, I listen for any overly long pauses that need to be tightened up, multiple takes that need to be eliminated, etc.

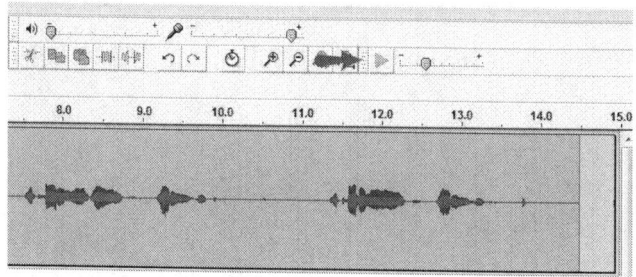

The first time I listen to the file I've recorded, I do it at a sped-up pace. In the Audacity Transcription Toolbar you'll see a slider control for Playback Speed. This allows you to change the speed of what you're listening to, faster or slower. This serves a number of purposes. First of all, it saves you time. Even though you'll be stopping and starting and deleting audio, you'll find you can edit the whole file in about the same amount of time it took you to record it. Second, it can help give you some distance from the sound of your own voice. Since anyone's sped up voice sounds nothing like them and even a bit ridiculous (somewhat like Alvin and the Chipmunks if you remember them), it also helps you to lighten up. Third, since you'll be listening to all the words at normal speed in the Second Edit, it helps ease the tediousness of the process. And finally, it will help you concentrate and pay attention to the words. Otherwise, you can tend to zone out a bit and miss something.

I've found the optimal speed for my First Edit playback is about 1.8x. Your results may vary. If you find it hard to follow along, try a lower setting at first and see if you can speed up over time.

So let's begin the First Edit. Place your manuscript, whether on your tablet or as a hard copy, where you can see both it and your computer screen. After you've adjusted your Playback Speed, begin playing your file by hitting the Play Button or hitting the spacebar, and follow along. When you get to a spot that needs to be deleted, such as a portion of a very long pause or somewhere that you read the words more than once, stop the playback by hitting the Stop Button or hitting the spacebar again. Highlight the section you want to delete in the Track Control Panel using your mouse and hit the delete key on your keyboard.

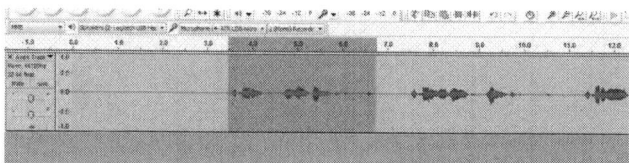

Poof! It's gone. Don't worry, if you ever make a mistake you can always undo it by clicking Undo in the Edit menu or hitting Ctrl+Z on your keyboard. After you delete a piece of audio, use your mouse to click on a point a couple seconds before the edit point in the Track Control Panel (just to make sure you didn't delete anything you didn't want to) and begin listening again.

Sometimes you'll find a place in your file that needs to be rerecorded entirely and you'll need to perform a pickup. Unlike editing a word processing file, you can't just replace a word when you've used it wrong. First of all, it wouldn't sound right. No matter how good you are, it ends up sounding like one of those awful automated voicemail prompts you "customize." You know the ones: "You've reached the voicemail box of...JIM JOHNSON...please leave a message..." It stands out like a sore thumb. The other, more important reason you can't just replace a word or two, is that audio simply doesn't look like that. The sounds of speech ebb and flow into each other and it's nearly impossible to pick out individual words on an audio track. Instead, you'll need to re-record an isolated phrase, one with natural pauses in speech both before and after.

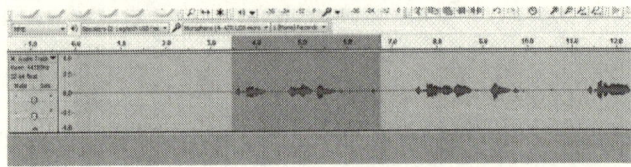

So listen to your recording, find an appropriate phrase to replace, and make note of it in your manuscript. Hit Mute in the original audio track in the Track Control Panel so you don't hear the playback as you're recording. Go back to your microphone with your manuscript and place yourself in the same configuration as when you recorded the track. Hit the Record Button or R on your keyboard and record the line. (Audacity will record the pickup in a second track below your original track.) Try delivering your pickup phrase a few times in a row to get the read you want. Try to match your original cadence as much as possible.

When you have a take you're happy with, hit the Stop Button or the spacebar to stop recording. Listen back to your pickups and pick the phrase you like best. Highlight it using the mouse and select Copy from the Edit menu or Ctrl+C. Close the second track by hitting the X in the upper left corner of the track itself and unmute your original track. Highlight the original phrase you want to replace and select Paste from the Edit menu or Ctrl+V on your keyboard. Use your mouse to click on a point a couple seconds before the edit point in the Track Control Panel and listen to make sure you're happy with the edit. Then continue listening to the rest of the file.

When you reach the end of the file, you're almost done with the First Edit. ACX asks you to leave .5 seconds at the beginning of your file, 2.5 seconds between the chapter title and the first line of the chapter itself, and 3.5 seconds at the end of the chapter. Delete any excess audio to get close to these times, leaving about an extra half second in each spot. In the Second Edit they'll be easier to see and we'll tweak them exactly.

Finally, save the file.

The Second Edit – Mastering

After you've completed your First Edit for Quality Control to ensure that all the words in your book are there (and nothing else), it's time to take a second editing pass to improve the audio quality of the final product.

First, save a second copy of the file using Save Project As under the File menu, adding "Post" to the end of the filename. This will ensure that if you really screw up something in the Mastering step, you can still go back to your unaltered file.

Noise Reduction

First we'll address background noise. Ideally your computer should be placed a fair distance away from your microphone, maybe even in another room, to avoid picking up the noise of the fan. But I don't live in a perfect world and neither, probably, do you. I have a small corner of a room to serve all my computing and sound recording needs. As a result, my microphone sits fairly near my computer, so the sound of the fan leaves a telltale regular hum in the background. (And there's other background noise as well, from street noise transmitted through windows, the sound of the ventilation system, even from compact fluorescent light bulbs.) This background noise is not that noticeable, but when we get to the compression step, we'll be amplifying the overall sound levels of the file a bit. And that means we'll be amplifying the background noise as well if we don't address it. Fortunately, because the sound of a computer fan is constant and regular, we can easily eliminate it using Audacity's Noise Reduction function.

This is where those "empty" seconds at the end of the audio file will come in handy. This is what's known in the business as "room tone," the background noise in the room when you aren't speaking. This room tone will allow us to isolate the sound profile of the background noise that we want to eliminate.

The Noise Reduction function is a two-step process. Using your mouse, highlight a few seconds at the end of the audio in the Track Control Panel. Then click on Noise Reduction under the Effect menu and click on the Get Noise Profile Button under Step 1.

Next highlight all the audio in the track by clicking anywhere in the gray area to the left of the audio track itself. Then click on Noise Reduction under the Effect menu again, and enter the following settings under Step 2:

Noise Reduction 6 dB

Sensitivity 6.00

Frequency Smoothing 6

Noise Remove

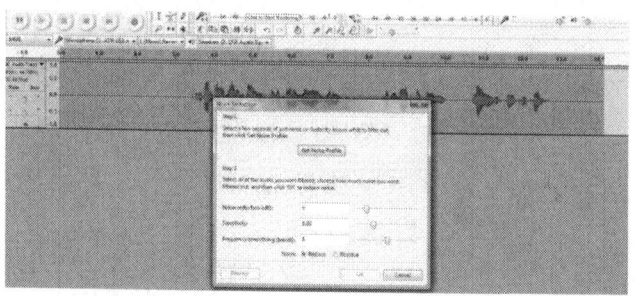

Compression and RMS Calculation

Now it's time to perform that compression step I spoke of earlier. Compression is a method of processing audio in order to even out the overall volume of a recording. A dynamic processor will reduce the volume of loud portions of the recording and raise the level of quiet portions. This makes for a better listening experience, one in which the listener does not have to adjust the volume of their device up and down.

For compression, I use Chris's Dynamic Compressor, the plug-in I had you install in the chapter on setting up Audacity. (To go into why the particular settings shown here were chosen is beyond the scope of this book. For more details, go the website for The Audacity to Podcast, at theaudacitytopodcast.com and listen to episodes TAP005 and TAP065.)

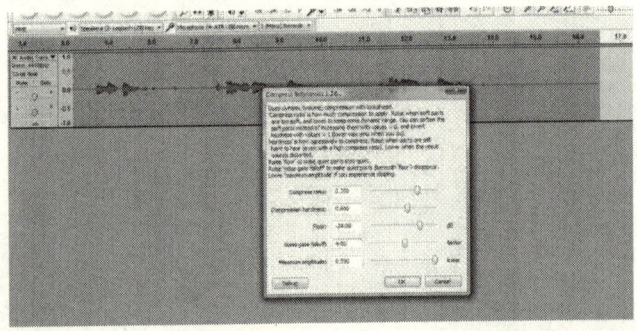

With the entire audio track still highlighted, click on Compress Dynamics 1.2.6 under the Effect menu, and enter the following settings:

Compress Ratio .75

Compression Hardness .6

Floor -24

Noise Gate Falloff 4.0

Maximum Amplitude .99

Then click OK.

Next we want to check the sound levels of our file to see if our compressor did the job. (Don't freak out, we're going to get a little technical here.) We do this by looking at the RMS, or Root Mean Square levels of the file. This is a complicated mathematical function, but to oversimplify, the RMS is the average sound level of all those squiggly peaks and valleys, measured in decibels, or dB.

ACX requires the RMS to fall between -23dB and -18dB, with a target of RMS -20dB. (When using a digital audio editor such as Audacity, dB refers to the sound level relative to the full scale or Decibels Full Scale (dBFS). That means when you refer to the decibel level of your recording, 0dB is at the top of the scale, or the loudest level. As the sound level gets quieter, it goes down the scale, becoming a greater and greater negative value. So in the ACX standard, for example, -18dB is 5 decibels louder than -23dB.)

To check the RMS, I use RMS Calculate, the second plug-in I had you install in the chapter on setting up Audacity. To see if the RMS of the file meets ACX standards, click RMS Calculate under the Analyze menu.

I look for the calculated RMS of the audio file to fall between -20.1dB and -19.9dB. This ensures the same sound level from chapter to chapter. If the RMS calculated is outside this range, then "Undo" RMS Calculate and "Undo" the Compressor under the Edit menu or hit Ctrl+Z on your keyboard twice. Click on Compress Dynamics 1.2.6 under the Effect menu and adjust the Compressor Ratio setting up or down as needed. Then click OK and compress again. Next click RMS Calculate under the Analyze menu again to check RMS.

Repeat the compression and RMS steps as needed until the RMS falls between -20.1dB and -19.9dB. (This is an iterative process you'll get used to and is not as convoluted as it sounds.)

Hard Limiting

Next, run the Hard Limiter. ACX requires all uploaded files to be hard limited so there are no peak values higher than -3.0dB. Hard limiting clips off any peaks that might create distortion.

With the entire audio track still highlighted, click on Limiter under the Effect menu, choose Hard Limit as the type, and move the Limit To slider until it reads -3.0dB. Then click OK.

Save the file.

Playback

Now listen to the whole chapter again, as a final quality check to make sure everything sounds good. Listen at regular speed without your manuscript in front of you to best simulate how a listener would hear the audiobook. Also, take this opportunity to remove any breaths and pops that are distracting and adjust pauses as needed. This is a judgment call. Some people suggest leaving breaths in to make the recording sound more natural, but if you listen to a professionally produced audiobook, you'll rarely hear them. And even if you decide to leave "normal" breaths in, I still think you'll find some breaths that come at very unnatural places. To eliminate a breath, grab a very short piece of audio from the "room tone" portion of your recording by highlighting about a quarter second and copying it. When you find a breath, highlight it and then paste your room tone over it. To eliminate small pops or lip smacks, zoom in on the offending spike in the Audacity Edit Toolbar, highlight as little of the spike as possible, and then delete it. (You can perform very fine highlighting by clicking on the audio track in the Track Control Panel, and then holding the Shift key while hitting the Left and Right arrow keys on your keyboard.)

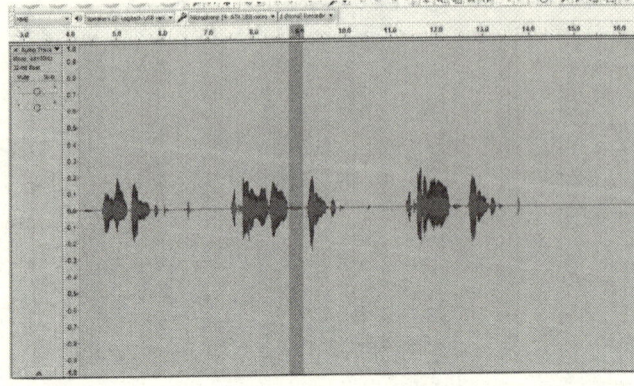

When you reach the end of the file, you're almost done with the Second Edit. ACX asks you to leave .5 seconds at the beginning of your file, 2.5 seconds between the chapter title and the first line of the chapter itself, and 3.5 seconds at the end of the chapter. Delete any excess audio to get to these times.

Finally, save the file.

Exporting the File

When I'm finally happy with the file, I export it as an mp3. Click on Export Audio under the File menu. Set the Save As Type to mp3. Next, click on the Options Button and make sure the Bit Rate Mode is set to Constant, the Quality is set to 192 kbps, and the Channel Mode is Joint Stereo. Delete the word "Post" from the file name, and click Save.

Putting Your Audiobook Together

Repeat the recording and two-step editing process for each chapter of your book. At the end of the recording process, you should have as many files as you have chapters. But there are three more files ACX requires you to create before your work is done. These three files are Opening Credits, Closing Credits, and a Retail Sample.

ACX suggests a standard format for Opening and Closing Credits, which works nicely. For example, if your name was Joe Blow and the book you copyrighted in 2012 and recorded in 2015 is entitled *The Great American Novel*, for your Opening Credits you would record the following phrase:

"The Great American Novel, written by Joe Blow, Narrated by Joe Blow."

And for the Closing Credits you would record:

"This has been, The Great American Novel, written by Joe Blow, narrated by Joe Blow. Copyright 2012 by Joe Blow, Production Copyright 2015 by Joe Blow."

To save time, I usually record the Closing Credits, completely edit the file, and export it. I then save the same file as the Opening Credits and edit out the "This has been" and copyright information, and then export the file. Granted, it doesn't save a lot of time, but every minute counts.

The final file you have to create is your Retail Sample. When you go to Amazon, iTunes, or Audible, there will be a short sample of the audiobook available so folks can listen and see if they want to buy it. The Retail Sample needs to be less than five minutes, so unless your chapters are very short, you'll probably need to choose an excerpt.

Don't make the mistake of automatically choosing the first five minutes of your book and calling it good. Consider a passage that will grab the listener's attention and make them want to hear more. In many cases, a typical fiction book will start with exposition or some kind of set-up scene before getting into the action. And a lot of nonfiction starts with "Why I Wrote This Book" or "Who am I and Why Should You Listen to Me" information.

Instead, for a fiction book, look for a scene early in the book with crackling dialogue that shows off your writing style, or an action scene that leaves the listener wondering what comes next. Don't worry too much about whether they have all the context they need to understand it – just try to grab the listener. Similarly, for nonfiction, give them some information that immediately helps them solve a problem related to the main topic of your book. Or take an excerpt from a chapter that speaks to the problems they face and how you are going to solve them. In short, offer value to the listener and they'll want more.

In order to keep your Retail Sample under five minutes, you probably aren't going to be able to present a complete scene, section, or chapter, but make sure your excerpt ends on the conclusion of a thought, even if you have to make it a few seconds shorter than five minutes.

When all your files are complete and exported to mp3, log on to ACX and click on the Projects menu at the top left of the screen. Then locate the project for your book and upload each of the mp3 audio files one by one, following the directions. When you are done, submit your files to ACX. And that's it. It will take a week or two for your book to be available for sale and ACX will determine the sales price. Later, ACX should also send you some free product codes for you to raffle or give away to members of your mailing list or to reviewers. Use these wisely for marketing and watch your sales increase.

How to Read Like a Pro

The first thing to realize when attempting to record your manuscript is that audio is an extremely intimate medium. If you think about how people will listen to your audiobook, many times it will be through ear buds or headphones. This means you will literally be whispering in their ear. So when it's time to read, don't think of yourself as an announcer or newsreader. If you've ever given a speech or performed on stage, don't think of it as playing to the 42nd row. If you've done a reading at a book shop, don't think about it as addressing an audience of people. The single most effective way to give a good audiobook performance is to tell a story to one person. In fact, take this a step farther, and think about telling the story to one specific person. Think about your ideal audience member. And not an idealized abstraction, but a real person.

Let your physicality help you as well. You'll want to have good posture, of course, since you'll be spending hours reading from the same position. And good posture will lead to good breath control, a must. So sit up straight, but keep your body relaxed. If you keep your posture too stiff and formal, you run the risk of it coloring your performance, making you sound a bit pedantic or academic. Take on a natural posture, one that's comfortable. And then lean slightly into the microphone. This will affect your performance subconsciously. You will naturally drop your volume a bit, and become more intimate, which is what we want.

You see, in addition to any actual characters you may be playing in your book (more on that later), you're also taking on one additional character: the narrator. It is not just you reading the words on a page, but rather a specific person that is telling this story, whether your book is written in the first person or the third. If you are reading a nonfiction book, you are also taking on a character, the person who is imparting the information, again regardless of whether it is in the first or third person.

You will also be playing other characters throughout the course of your read. If you are reading fiction, you'll be playing different people, men and women, with various ages and backgrounds from all walks of life. If you are reading nonfiction, you may not be taking on other characters per se. For example, if you're reading a manual about How to Record Your Own Audiobook, you may never switch from the role of "narrator." But even in books like these, there are often subtle opportunities to take on other characters, such as when you quote an expert, or present an excerpt from another source. This is an ideal time for you to add a bit of variety to what otherwise could become a monotonous experience for the listener. So let's talk about character.

How to Create Characters

Naturally, this applies more to fiction than nonfiction. When your listener is tuned into your audiobook, you want to find every way you can to keep them in the story. So as your book progresses, if you read a line of dialogue and the listener starts thinking, "Wait, which character is this speaking now?" you've lost them. Additionally, there's the disadvantage we face because character attributions often come at the end of lines of dialogue rather than at the beginning. So an author will usually write: "I can't let you go out on a night like this," Sally said. This works perfectly well in print since most of us unconsciously scan ahead as we're reading, or easily backfill character once we realize who it was who said a line. But in audio, your story is literally being delivered one word at a time. There is no scanning ahead and no chance to look back at what was said. The words keep coming relentlessly, one after the other. In a good way, of course.

If you want an example of great characterization, I suggest listening to a few of the top readers on Audible. In most cases, you can listen to a five minute sample absolutely free. Or you could join Audible and get a free audiobook of your choice. Or go to your local library and check out a few titles on CD for free. (Or, heaven forbid, you could buy an audiobook.) The audiobook industry has its own set of superstars, folks like Scott Brick, Hillary Huber, Dick Hill, and Simon Vance. One of my personal favorites is Jim Dale reading the Harry Potter books. There are literally hundreds of characters introduced over the course of the seven Harry Potter books (a reported 134 in *Harry Potter and the Order of the Phoenix* alone), and Jim does such a good job that you are never in doubt of exactly which character is speaking at any given time. And he does it in such a non-showy way. His characters are real people, not caricatures, no mean feat when voicing wizards, witches, and mythical creatures.

So take a page from Jim's book when creating characters. A lot of them are based on people he knows – an old comedian friend or a favorite aunt. He records a snippet of dialogue for each character on a microcassette recorder so he can listen to it for reference when recording, but you could just as easily jot down reminders in a little notebook (Detective McSweeney = Uncle John after a few drinks). You may think you'll remember what voice you did previously, but believe me when I tell you, you won't. It is easy to get confused, especially when recording chapters days apart.

To get started on a pool of characters you can draw upon later, make a list of your relatives and friends who you've interacted with often enough to instantly recall how they sound. Ideal candidates would be those family members and acquaintances that you actually "do" at parties or get-togethers. You know the ones – the real "characters" that you tell stories about: "So Uncle Fred says to the grocer, 'You're just gonna throw those grapes out. I'll give ya a dollar for the bunch!'" Go through each person on the list and highlight those that come to you the easiest and seem to represent a very specific stereotype.

Next, make a list of celebrities that you know well with a very specific persona, the ones you follow on the gossip websites or the ones for whom you see every movie or television show they do. While you're brainstorming here, also consider the characters these actors play in movies and on TV that you can draw upon. Think about stereotypes: The dastardly villainess from your favorite soap, the blowhard know-it-all from your favorite sitcom, the world-weary detective from your favorite police procedural. Again, the more time you've spent watching and absorbing their traits, the better. And if you feel like you've never actively observed characters with an eye for detail, now is the perfect time to start. It will turn your "vegging out in front of the TV time" into "productive research time" in no time.

Now look to other sources of character voices. What about the cashier at your grocery store? The candidate on the political ads running every 15 minutes? That perky meteorologist on the news? The voices you do when reading your child's favorite bedtime story? These are all sources of characters for your master list.

But we're not done yet. We can still flavor these characters and alter them to create new, unique characters. You see, you don't have to be a perfect mimic to use voices from real life. In fact, it's better if you aren't. If you do a pitch-perfect Christopher Walken impersonation, that's a lot of fun at parties, but you shouldn't use that voice for a character in your book. The last thing you want the listener to think when hearing you perform the police captain in your novel is, "Wow! He sounds just like Christopher Walken!" It will take the reader out of the book and break the narrative dream. So what can you do?

Well, you have a lot of weapons in your arsenal to change and color voices. You can change the pace of the base character's speech, making it faster or slower than normal. You can change the vocal range of the character, having them speak in a higher-pitched or lower-pitched tone. You can give qualities to their voice like graveliness or breathiness or nasaliness. So take that Christopher Walken impression, raise the pitch and add some breathiness, and it might be just perfect for that quirky femme fatale.

Other Tips

Remember, you will be editing your recording, so use this to your advantage. Sometimes even as a sentence is escaping our lips, we know that we're performing it wrong. If you're like me, if you attempt to go on and hope it's okay, it will be there in the back of your mind, bugging you. This will take you out of the moment and affect your read, maybe even causing you to screw up again. Better to bite the bullet and record the line again.

Along those same lines, in order to get the read you want for a given line, you can "warm up" with a sound or phrase which you'll edit out later. So if you want to deliver a line lightheartedly, laugh aloud and then deliver the line. Later, just delete the laugh itself and leave the line following it. Other "warm ups" include sighing, gasping, or saying the words, "Hey," "Oh," or "Ugh," to name just a few.

Also, if you have trouble switching between two characters, then take a second or two to regroup. Later, you can edit that second or two out.

Sometimes there will be a sentence or short phrase that you're just not sure how best to read. You can use an old voiceover technique I've used in professional recording sessions called "Three Wild." This means reading the same line three times in a row, in three completely different ways. Play with tone, emphasis, cadence, etc. And have fun, knowing you're going to throw two of them away. Let's say the phrase in question is a character saying, "Oh, is it?" You might read it once dryly, then with great anticipation, then matter-of-factly. But don't be this calculating about it. Instead, just try to do it a different way each time, without overthinking it. And if you want to try a fourth or fifth way, that's cool, too.

Sometimes a line of dialogue that looks just fine on the page – and is perfectly fine if you're silently reading in your head – can become a tongue-twisting minefield when trying to read it aloud. You trip over a word. So you start over and trip over the same word. Now you're getting a bit frustrated, so you start again and trip over an even earlier word. Don't let this get to you. It happens to all of us. Just take a deep breath and try to do the sentence in an entirely new manner. Slow it down a bit and find a non-intuitive yet natural place to add a pause as you read. Usually the problem lies in trying to run too many words together. If you're really stuck – as when reading an unfamiliar foreign phrase or the name of a chemical or a real tongue twister – you may have to actually take non-natural pauses between individual words, which you will remove later in editing. If you have to do this, try to still read each word with the tone and inflection you would use if they were all strung together. Then when you take out the pauses, it will not sound perfect, but relatively natural.

In general, slow down. We all tend to read aloud just a bit too fast, like it's a timed competition. Remember you're telling a story. And your listener can't go back and scan something they missed as they can in print. Let the story unfold. Keep in mind you are dramatizing a narrative, not simply reading words on a page. And yes, this applies to nonfiction as well.

Sometimes you may not know how a word is pronounced, even a word you wrote yourself. Proper nouns are especially prone to being used in writing without necessarily knowing how they're pronounced. This is when you realize how different the written word is from the spoken. The easiest way I have found to find pronunciations is to simply go to Google and type "pronounce" followed by the word in question. So if, for example, you need to know how to say the word "mnemonic," type "pronounce mnemonic" in Google. The top results will take you to a number of websites with short videos or audio clips you can play to hear the pronunciation. This also works like a dream for foreign words, names, and places. Using the "pronounce" search term will take you to websites where you'll hear a number of samples from native speakers.

Finally, Undo is your friend when using Audacity. If you make a mistake when editing, or delete a piece of audio you didn't mean to, or applied an effect ineffectively, just click on Undo under the Edit menu or hit Ctrl+Z on your keyboard. It's like it never happened.

So Long, Stressed-Out Writer

The recording and editing process I've outlined may seem complicated at first, but trust me, it becomes easier with repetition. Just go back over the material and take it one step at a time. You'll quickly go from being overwhelmed to the production process becoming second nature.

The method I've presented here certainly isn't the only way to produce a quality audiobook, but it's consistently worked for me. If you find any improvements of your own to this process – or if you have an idea for another topic you'd like to see become part of the Stressed-Out Writer's Guide Series – please contact me at www.kirkhanley.com and let me know. I'd love to hear from you. And while you're at my website, please consider signing up for my free email updates.

Thank you for buying the book, and best of luck to you in all your endeavors!

Resources

Here are some helpful resources to advance your voice-over education.

ACX

www.acx.com

Start your education here. ACX has a great website, full of useful information and encouragement. You'll find videos to help you learn more about editing and recording, the technical specs required for the final product, and tips on marketing. Also, if you've recorded a book or two of your own and would like to try your hand at auditioning for other authors, you can search for titles accepting auditions. If nothing else, you'll get a chance to see the books others are putting onto the market and even get some helpful examples – both good and bad – of how to create and market a self-published book. Additionally, ACX has a blog where they offer links to interesting articles, profiles of authors and producers, and tips on recording and equipment.

The Creative Penn

www.thecreativepenn.com

Not a voiceover website, per se, Joanna Penn is an absolute must-read for the world of being a self-published author – or an author entrepreneur, as Joanna might put it. Joanna also likes to live on the bleeding edge of publishing, translating her books into other languages and creating audiobooks, both through ACX and recording them herself for sale on her website.

Edge Studio's Whittam's World

www.youtube.com/user/edgestudiovoiceover

So many voiceover experts, especially the tech guys, seem to live in another world, one of jargon-filled explanations, unlimited resources to buy equipment, and striving to create the perfect world, free of noise. Not so George Whittam. He speaks in plain English, and understands the concept of "good enough" when it comes to the world of voiceover. You'll get practical, actionable tips as George answers listeners' questions in a refreshing, clear way. Highly recommended.

Screen Actors Guild Foundation "How to Get Paid for Reading Books"

www.youtube.com/watch?v=GIgk7O8l4g0

This is a great open discussion with Jason Ojalvo, Vice President of Audible, and three giants of the audiobook industry – Scott Brick, Hillary Huber, and Pat Fraley – folks who have recorded and produced hundreds of books between them. In the second half of the video, they coach performers on their technique, giving them direction and pointers that will be helpful to any audiobook narrator.

The Audacity to Podcast

theaudacitytopodcast.com

It can be hard to find info online pertinent to audiobook performing and production, so here's a tip: Look for info about podcasting instead. Podcasting and audiobook production have more in common than separates them. And one of the best places to get info on podcasting and Audacity software is this website. Be sure to check out the info on Chris's Dynamic Compressor in podcasts TAP005 and TAP065, which give more details on how to arrive at the proper settings than I could share in this book.

Audacity Website

www.audacityteam.org

The place to download Audacity, but there is also an online user manual and much, much more. Time spent here getting familiar with the resources available will yield dividends later.

Audacity Forum

forum.audacityteam.org

A message board with a lot of good info, searchable by topic. It's a great place to turn when you're wondering how to use a certain feature or unsure how to get the results you want. I admit sometimes the discussions do go a bit over my head, but for the most part they are a friendly bunch. If you'd like to know more, join, post a question, and get involved.

Pat Fraley

patfraley.com

In addition to being an experienced audiobook narrator and producer himself, Pat offers eCourses, live instruction, and coaching services. A very encouraging, supportive, and knowledgeable teacher, I can unequivocally recommend following Pat and purchasing his materials.

AudioFile Magazine

www.audiofilemagazine.com

The website for AudioFile magazine, with industry news, narrator profiles, reviews, and more.

AudioFile Magazine Digital Editions

digital.audiofilemagazine.com

Actual issues of AudioFile Magazine in a digital format, free to read online. Inside, you'll find Audiobook industry news, reviews of new audiobooks, and audio samples. Well worth a monthly visit.

Glossary

Artifact: Undesirable sound in a recording. Sometimes artifacts can be introduced through poor audio editing, which may create sounds or qualities not present in the original recording.

Audiobook: The audio version of a printed manuscript, read by one or more narrators. Typically supplied in a number of individual files, one for each chapter, plus files for the Opening Credits and Closing Credits.

Clipping: When sound level exceeds a system's capability to capture it, it will be clipped. In digital recording, such as when using Audacity, this can happen when the peak digital signal exceeds 0dBFS (Decibels Full Scale) or, in other words, the top of the dB scale. A clipped signal may sound distorted and displeasing to the ear. Clipping can be avoided by adjusting the input signal level prior to recording.

Compression: A method of processing audio in order to even out the overall volume of a recording. A dynamic processor will reduce the volume of loud portions of the recording and raise the level of quiet portions. This makes for a better listening experience, one in which the listener does not have to adjust the volume of the device up and down.

Digital Audio Workstation (DAW): An electronic tool or software program for recording, editing, producing, and playback of digital audio. Audacity is an example of a DAW.

Decibel (dB): The standard unit of measurement of the "loudness" of a sound, used to represent sound volume or sound level. When using a digital audio editor, such as Audacity, dB refers to the sound level relative to the full scale or Decibels Full Scale (dBFS). That means when expressing the decibel level of your recording, 0dB is at the top of the scale, or the loudest level, and as the sound level gets quieter, it goes down the scale, becoming a greater and greater negative value.

Distortion: When the audio input exceeds a speaker's or headphones' capacity of output, distortion can result.

Dynamic Range: The difference in decibels between the loudest undistorted level of a recording and the noise floor.

Encoding: Converting uncompressed audio files into a compressed format (usually mp3) when the final audiobook files are exported.

Equalization (EQ): Increasing, decreasing, or eliminating audio frequency ranges to improve the sound of an audio recording.

Frequency: The number of cycles per second of an audio signal's sine wave. The audio frequency range for human hearing is generally 20 Hz to 20,000 Hz. Generally speaking, the higher the frequency, the higher in pitch we hear the sound.

Headroom: The difference between the maximum sound level of a given recording and the maximum operating level of an audio system, usually 0dB. ACX asks producers to hard limit their recording to -3dB, giving 3dB of headroom. This gives a factor of safety so any post-processing will not cause the recording to exceed 0dB.

Level: The average volume of a recording.

Mastering: Processing raw audio to improve the characteristics of the sound file. It may involve compression, hard limiting, equalization, noise removal, and anything else that will make for a better listening experience.

Mono: Single-channel sound playback. Using headphones, both ears hear the same sound.

MP3: A standard audio format for audiobooks, podcasts, and digital music, able to be played on a wide variety of players and programs. Audio is compressed to reduce the file size, while retaining quality sound.

Narrator: The performer reading the audiobook.

Noise Floor: An audio level below the lowest level of the recording itself. Anything below the noise floor is considered background noise or room tone.

Noise Reduction (NR): Processing the audio to remove or lower background noise.

Normalize: A process to increase the volume of all audio by the same amount.

Producer: In ACX terminology, the person or company who will narrate, edit, master, and output the final audio files for a manuscript.

Raw Audio: The audio as it has been recorded, before any editing or mastering has taken place.

Root Mean Square (RMS): A mathematical calculation giving you the average volume level of an audio file.

Room Tone: The background noise in a room, ideally as quiet as possible. It is good to have a few seconds of room tone in your recording to use during editing.

Stereo: Dual-channel sound playback. A left signal is broadcast to the left speaker or headphone earpiece, and a right signal to the right.

WAV: The most common uncompressed audio format. (Editing and Mastering should always be performed on an uncompressed file.)

About the Author

For over fifteen years, Kirk was a part of famed comedy theatre, The Second City, working as a performer, writer, improviser, producer, director, teacher, and improv workshop facilitator. He co-wrote and performed in three national touring shows, one of which won an award for writing from Michigan's Oakland Press.

Kirk has also performed in children's theatre, outreach programs for teens, industrial stage shows, improvisational comedy revues, television and radio commercials, and corporate training films. He's written one-act plays for dinner theatre, online video scripts, and been a contributing writer for The Onion News Network.

Kirk now lives in Virginia with his wife Deborah where he writes, coaches comedy writers, and narrates audiobooks.

To find out more about Kirk and sign up for his free email updates, please go to www.kirkhanley.com.

Made in the USA
San Bernardino, CA
30 March 2019